Mallorca

Travel Guide

2023

A comprehensive guide to Mallorca first time visitors: What to discover, where to visit, how to prepare and experience the beautiful culture of the people on the Island.

By

Jolida Travels

TABLE OF CONTENT

COPYRIGHT

INTRODUCTION

Overview of Mallorca

When to Travel

Getting There

I.

GETTING AROUND

Public Transportation Options

Accommodations \ Hotels

Resorts

Holiday Rentals

II:

FOOD AND DRINK

Traditional Cuisine

Native Specialities

Prestigious Eateries and Bars

III:

ATTRACTIONS AND ACTIVITIES

Beaches and Water Sports

Cultural and Historical Landmarks

Entertainment and Nightlife

Shopping

Designer Boutiques

IV:

PRACTICAL INFORMATION

Currency and Money Exchange

Language

Safety Advice

CONCLUSION

Final Thoughts

INTRODUCTION

Overview of Mallorca

The biggest island in the Balearic Islands, Mallorca, usually referred to as Majorca, is situated in the Mediterranean Sea off the eastern coast of Spain. The island, which has a population of around 900,000, is well-known as a tourist destination because of its lovely beaches, breathtaking natural scenery, and rich cultural history.

The dynamic and active city of Palma, Mallorca's capital, is home to a magnificent Gothic cathedral, a medieval fortress, and a wide variety of museums and art galleries. Moreover, Palma is home to several eateries, cafés, and bars that provide a wide range of food and nightlife alternatives.

Beachgoers and outdoor lovers will find Mallorca to be the perfect vacation location because of its warm, sunny weather. The island is home to various parks and environmental reserves, as well as the Serra de Tramuntana mountain range. The beaches on the island vary from quiet coves to long, sandy lengths.

Mallorca has a rich cultural past in addition to its natural beauty, with several historical monuments and cultural landmarks dispersed all across the island. In addition to museums and galleries presenting the island's art, history, and culture, they include historical sites from antiquity, medieval castles, and traditional villages.

Everyone can find something to enjoy in Mallorca, from beachgoers and outdoor enthusiasts to history fans and cultural seekers. The island is varied and interesting.

When to Travel

The activities and sights you wish to see during your vacation will determine the ideal time to visit Mallorca. Mallorca has scorching summers and mild winters because to its Mediterranean environment. The many seasons are described below:

Spring (March to May): The weather is temperate and pleasant throughout the spring, with temperatures ranging from 15 to 25 degrees Celsius (59 to 77 degrees Fahrenheit). This is an excellent time to visit the island since it is less busy and offers a more sedate vacation.

Summer (June to August): With temperatures averaging approximately 30°C (86°F) and a hot, sunny climate, summer is Mallorca's busiest travel season. While it might be quite busy at the resorts and beaches, this is also a perfect time to engage in outdoor activities and water sports.

Autumn (September to November): Mallorca's autumn is temperate and pleasant, with temperatures averaging 15 to 25 degrees Celsius (59 to 77 degrees Fahrenheit). The island is less congested than it is in the summer, and the warm sea makes it a fantastic season for swimming and other water activities.

Winter (December to February): Mallorca's winters are typically warm, with lows of 5 to 15 degrees Celsius (41 to 59 degrees Fahrenheit). While there is less activity on the island at this time, certain restaurants and attractions could be closed. The ideal seasons to visit Mallorca are spring and fall, when the weather is nice and there are less tourists around. The summer season is the most well-liked time to go to the beach, nevertheless.

Spring (March to May): If you want to avoid crowds and enjoy moderate weather, spring is a perfect season to visit Mallorca. The island is lush and green, and the terrain is covered with wildflowers. The weather is suitable for outdoor pursuits like cycling and hiking, and you can take part in cultural activities like Palma's Easter processions.

Summer (June to August): The summer months are Mallorca's busiest travel months, and July and August may be particularly congested. Given that the water is warm and the sun is out, this is the ideal time for beachgoers. Also, you may take in outdoor performances, festivals, and nightlife. Accommodations and activities should be booked in advance however, since they tend to sell out fast.

Autumn (September to November): If you want to enjoy mild weather without the crowds, autumn is a terrific season to visit Mallorca. You may still swim in the water and engage in outdoor pursuits like golfing, riding, and hiking. September and October are ideal months to visit the island's vineyards and sample its wines since these months coincide with the island's wine harvest.

Winter (December to February): Winter is Mallorca's least busy season. While the weather is often moderate, there may be sporadic rain and wind. Yet in January, you may take part in cultural activities like the Sant Antoni festival and Christmas markets. As the island is calm and empty, hiking and cycling are also enjoyable at this time.

Getting There

Depending on your location and budget, there are a number of methods to go to Mallorca, a well-liked tourist destination. This is a detailed itinerary for traveling to Mallorca:

Via Plane: Flying is the fastest and most convenient method to reach Mallorca. Palma de Mallorca Airport, the only significant airport on the island, is situated approximately 8 kilometers (5 miles) east of Palma. Several European destinations, including London, Paris, Berlin, and Madrid, are easily accessible from the airport thanks to frequent flights operated by well-known carriers like Ryanair, EasyJet, and Vueling.

You may take a bus or a cab from the airport to go to your island location. If you prefer to see the island alone, you may also hire a vehicle at the airport.

Via Ferry: You may also get to Mallorca by ferry if you're coming from Spain or a neighbouring nation. Mallorca is served by a number of ferry companies, including Balearia, Trasmediterranea, and Acciona. Ferry services are accessible from a number of ports, including Barcelona, Valencia, Ibiza, and Menorca.

The cost of a ferry ticket and the length of the trip depend on where you start, and tickets may be bought online or at the port. Whether you wish to get to the island in your own car or if you prefer a more picturesque approach, the boat is a terrific choice.

By Train: While the island of Mallorca lacks a railway system, it is nonetheless feasible to reach there by train from the Spanish mainland. The closest train station to Palma is in Valencia, where Renfe, the Spanish national railroad, runs frequent services.

You may go to Mallorca by connecting bus or boat from Valencia. Although while it could take longer than other possibilities, taking the train to the island is a relaxing and picturesque option.

By Car: You may also get to Mallorca by automobile if you're coming from the continent of Europe. Car ferries to Mallorca are run by a number of ferry companies from ports in Italy and Spain. While on the island, you may use your automobile to see its many landmarks and beaches.

It's crucial to remember that renting a vehicle is another common choice on the island. Many car rental firms are accessible at the airport and in main towns. Driving in Mallorca may be difficult, particularly during the busiest travel season, so make sure you are acquainted with the rules of the road.

By Bus: You may also get to Mallorca via bus if you're coming from the Spanish mainland. Services to Palma are provided by a number of bus operators, including Alsa and Eurolines. Depending on where you start, the travel duration varies, but it might be less expensive than using other forms of transportation.

You may take a cab or a local bus from Palma to any location on the island.

Depending on your location, financial situation, and tastes, there are a variety of methods to go to Mallorca. It's simple to get to Mallorca and there are several ways to get about, including driving, flying, and taking a boat.

I.

GETTING AROUND

Public Transportation Options

It is simple to tour Mallorca without a vehicle thanks to the island's effective public transit system that links the main cities and villages. This is a detailed overview of Mallorca's public transportation choices:

The most popular kind of public transportation in Mallorca is the bus, which is run by TIB (Transport de les

Illes Balears). The majority of the island is served by the bus network, which also offers regular service to tourist hotspots and significant cities.

Buses come in two varieties: interurban buses and urban buses. Although interurban buses link several towns and villages, urban buses run only inside the boundaries of Palma and other significant cities.

The buses are up-to-date, cozy, air-conditioned, and furnished with free Wi-Fi. The prices are reasonable; a single ticket will run you between 1.50

and 2 euros, depending on how far you go.

Tickets for buses may be purchased from the driver or from ticket vending machines at bus stops. It's crucial to remember that bus service in rural regions may be less frequent, so it's a good idea to check the schedule before making travel arrangements.

Trains: While Mallorca lacks a comprehensive rail system, there is a tourist train that runs between Palma and Soller. The Soller Train or Orange Express is a historic railway that travels through tunnels and beautiful landscapes.

The voyage, which lasts approximately an hour and travels through charming towns and villages, provides a unique approach to see the island's natural splendor. From March to November, the train runs every day. A one-way ticket costs around 18 euros, which is a reasonable price.

Moreover, a tram service with breathtaking views of the Mediterranean Sea travels between Soller and the port of Soller. The tram runs every day from March to

November and offers a contemporary, air-conditioned service.

Taxis: Taxis are generally accessible in Mallorca and a practical and economical means of short distance transport. In large towns and cities, taxis are available at taxi ranks, or they may be flagged down on the street.

The municipal government in Mallorca controls the rates for metered taxis. The prices are affordable, with an average trip from the airport to the heart of Palma costing between 20 and 25 euros.

It's crucial to remember that taxi costs might increase at night or during the busiest travel times, so it's a good idea to verify the fare before boarding the vehicle.

Vehicle rental: If you wish to go to isolated beaches and rural regions in Mallorca, this is a common alternative. There are several automobile rental firms with affordable prices at the airport and in significant towns and cities.

It's crucial to remember that driving in Mallorca may be tough, particularly during the busiest travel times when parking can be difficult to come by and the roads can be packed. Before driving in Mallorca, it is important to get acquainted with the local traffic rules and regulations.

The public transportation system in Mallorca is efficient and effective, providing cheap and practical ways to go about the island. There are several alternatives available, whether you want to commute by bus, rail, taxi, or rental vehicle.

choices for cycling and walking

Due to its breathtaking natural landscape, quaint communities, and varied terrain, Mallorca is a biker and walker's dream. Here is a detailed overview of Mallorca's riding and walking options:

Cycling: It's understandable why Mallorca is a favourite destination for bikers. The island offers a wide variety of bicycle routes, from peaceful rural lanes and scenic towns to mountain peaks and seaside highways.

In Mallorca, some of the most well-liked bicycle routes are as follows:

The Tramuntana Mountains: This mountain range provides some of Mallorca's most beautiful and difficult cycling routes. The views are breathtaking, with sweeping panoramas of the Mediterranean Sea and the craggy coastline, despite the tiny and twisting roads.

The Plains of Es Pla: With peaceful roads that meander through charming towns and farms, this flat, open area is ideal for pleasant riding.

The Coastline: There are many places to stop for a swim or a picnic along Mallorca's coastal roads, which provide some of the most spectacular views of the Mediterranean Sea.

On the island, there are several places to hire bikes, and the costs are affordable. In addition to providing bike rentals, several hotels and guesthouses also provide guided riding trips.

It's crucial to keep in mind that riding in Mallorca may be difficult, particularly during the summer when temperatures can skyrocket. It is essential to pack lots of water and food, as well as to dress appropriately.

Walking: The walking options in Mallorca are varied, ranging from simple seaside walks to strenuous mountain excursions. It is advisable to explore the island on foot to take in its breathtaking views of the sea, mountains, and farmland.

In Mallorca, some of the most well-liked walking paths are as follows:

There are several difficult and rewarding hiking paths in Mallorca's Serra de Tramuntana mountain range. With breath-taking vistas of the Mediterranean Sea, the routes travel through spectacular valleys, gorges, and mountains.

The Coastal Paths: Mallorca's coastline walkways provide short strolls with breathtaking sea views. The routes meander through hidden coves and beaches as they follow the rocky shoreline.

The Cami de Cavalls: This historic route circles the whole island and provides a unique approach to discover its breathtaking natural beauty. The route travels past charming towns, secluded bays, and craggy cliffs.

On the island, there are a number of guided walking excursions available, and several hotels and guesthouses provide maps and details on walking paths. Particularly during the heat, it's crucial to wear suitable footwear and have lots of water and food.

Another well-liked method of discovering Mallorca's natural beauty is on horseback. Several horseback riding facilities on the island provide guided trips through beautiful scenery and along the shore.

Both novice and expert riders may enjoy the rides at the horse-riding facilities, which provide well-trained horses and knowledgeable instructors.

It's crucial to keep in mind that horseback riding may be a difficult exercise, therefore it's recommended to dress appropriately and bring a lot of water and food.

Mallorca has a wide variety of bike, walking, and horseback riding possibilities, giving visitors lots of chances to see the island's stunning natural surroundings. There are several possibilities, whether you like a strenuous mountain trek, a relaxing coastline stroll, or a leisurely bike ride.

Accommodations \ Hotels

Mallorca is a well-liked vacation spot with a variety of lodging choices to fit every need and fancy. Below is a detailed list of some of Mallorca's top hotels:

Luxury Hotels: There are various luxury hotels in Mallorca, each of which provides a variety of facilities and services to make your stay pleasant and unforgettable. Some of Mallorca's top luxury hotels are listed below:

Belmond The Residence: The elegant hotel is situated in the little community of Deià, which is tucked away in the Serra de Tramuntana mountains. The hotel offers a spa, a variety of activities including culinary courses and art workshops, as well as breathtaking views of the Mediterranean Sea.

The St. Regis Mardavall Mallorca Resort is an opulent hotel with breathtaking views of the Mediterranean Sea. It is situated in the upscale marina of Puerto Portals. The hotel has a spa, a golf course, a number of dining options, and a selection of water activities.

Cap Rocat: Perched on a clifftop with a view of the Bay of Palma, this five-star hotel is housed in a historic military castle. The hotel offers breathtaking sea views, a spa, and a variety of activities including cycling and hiking.

Boutique Hotels: Mallorca is home to a variety of boutique hotels that provide a special and tailored experience. Some of Mallorca's top boutique hotels are listed below:

Hotel Sant Francesc Plural: The historic center of Palma is where this boutique hotel is housed in a 19th-century palace. The hotel has a restaurant, spa, and rooftop pool.

Hotel Can Mostatxins: In the picturesque town of Alcdia, in the island's north, is where you'll find this boutique hotel. The hotel has a variety of rooms and suites, as well as a pool and rooftop patio.

Among the Serra de Tramuntana mountains sits the boutique hotel known as Son Brull Hotel & Spa, which used to be a monastery. The hotel has a spa, a swimming pool, and a restaurant offering traditional food from Mallorca.

Hotels that welcome families: Mallorca is a well-liked vacation spot for families, and a variety of lodging options provide facilities and services for kids. The top hotels in Mallorca that welcome families are listed below:

Blue & Spa Viva: The resort town of Alcudia is home to this family-friendly hotel, which has a variety of kid-friendly features including a kids' club, a playground, and a water park.

The Fergus Style Cala Blanca Suites is a kid-friendly hotel with a kids' club, a playground, and a pool that is situated in the tourist destination of Santa Ponsa.

The Blau Colonia Sant Jordi Resort & Spa is a kid-friendly hotel with a kids' club, a playground, and a pool that is situated in the Colonia Sant Jordi community.

Hotels that are affordable: Mallorca is home to a number of hotels that are reasonably priced and provide guests with a pleasant stay. These are a few of Mallorca's top hotels that are reasonably priced:

Horizontal Hotel: The location of this inexpensive hotel on the hills above Palma provides breathtaking views of both the city and the ocean. It has a restaurant and a beautiful pool attached to it.

In the resort town of Cala d'Or, the Hotel Palladium is a reasonably priced lodging option that has a number of facilities including a pool, a restaurant, and a bar.

Hotel Baha Cala Ratjada: Located in the village of Cala Ratjada, this inexpensive hotel has a variety of facilities including a pool, a restaurant, and a bar.

Resorts

Mallorca, often called Majorca, is a well-liked vacation spot for tourists seeking warmth, beaches, and relaxation. The island is home to a broad variety of resorts, from fun party spots to quiet getaways. Below is a list of some of Mallorca's top resorts:

Magaluf: Situated in the southwest of Mallorca, Magaluf is a well-known tourist destination. It is renowned for having a vibrant nightlife with pubs and clubs. The major beach, Playa de Magaluf, is a broad expanse of golden sand that is surrounded by cafés and eateries. Young individuals and groups of friends looking for a vibrant and enjoyable vacation frequent the resort.

Palma Nova: Just adjacent to Magaluf lies the family-friendly vacation town of Palma Nova. With three beaches and shallow, tranquil seas, the resort is perfect for families with young children. In addition to having a wide selection of eateries, pubs, and stores, Palma Nova boasts excellent access to other areas of the island by public transportation.

Puerto Pollensa: In the north of Mallorca, there is a tranquil vacation community called Puerto Pollensa. It is well recognized for its gorgeous beaches, clean seas, and pine trees. The resort is well-liked by families and couples looking for a peaceful vacation since it features a variety of eateries, cafés, and stores.

Alcudia: Alcudia is a historic town in the north of Mallorca with a selection of lodging options to fit every price range. Beach de Alcudia, the resort's expansive sandy beach, is great for families with young children. With its winding lanes, classic structures, and historic ruins, Alcudia's old town is definitely worth exploring.

Cala Millor: Cala Millor is a well-known tourist destination on the island of Mallorca. The resort boasts a lengthy sandy beach that is surrounded by eateries, bars, and stores. Families and couples enjoy Cala Millor, which offers a variety of lodging alternatives to fit all price ranges.

Port de Pollença: In the north of Mallorca, Port de Pollença is a well-liked resort community with a selection of hotels, apartments, and villas. The resort has a large, sandy beach that is dotted with cafes and restaurants and offers a variety of water sports. Families and couples looking for a quiet and calm vacation frequent Port de Pollença.

Santa Ponsa is a well-known tourist destination on the southwest coast of Mallorca. The resort boasts a lengthy sandy beach that is surrounded by eateries, bars, and stores. Families and young individuals looking for a colorful and enjoyable holiday frequent Santa Ponsa.

Palma: Tourists looking for culture, history, and entertainment often go to Mallorca's capital city of Palma. There are hotels, flats, and hostels throughout the city to accommodate all price ranges. There are many things to do in Palma, such as see its magnificent cathedral, historic castles, museums, and lively nightlife.

Cala d'Or: In the southeast of Mallorca, Cala d'Or is a tranquil and lovely resort community. The resort offers a variety of sandy beaches with restaurants and cafes along their edges. Families and couples seeking a tranquil vacation frequent Cala d'Or.

There are resorts in Mallorca to suit every taste and price range. Mallorca offers it all, whether you're looking for a fun party location, a family-friendly resort, or a tranquil getaway.

Holiday Rentals

Holidaymakers looking for a variety of lodging alternatives, including vacation rentals, often go to Mallorca. There are many vacation rentals in Mallorca to suit all tastes and budgets, ranging from apartments and villas to farms and country estates.

This is a list of some of Mallorca's top holiday rentals:

Families and groups of friends looking for a large, private lodging option often choose villas. In Mallorca, there are several villas to choose from, ranging in size from personal and tiny to spacious and opulent. Villas are the perfect choice for travelers looking for a peaceful and private getaway since they often come with private swimming pools, gardens, and outdoor eating spaces.

Apartments: For couples and small families looking for a more convenient and economical lodging alternative, apartments are a popular choice. Mallorca offers a wide selection of flats, from modest studios to expansive mansions. As apartments often include kitchens, they are perfect for travelers who want to prepare their own meals.

Farmhouses: Those looking for a classic and rustic lodging alternative often choose farms, or fincas as they are called in Mallorca. Many farmhouses have been transformed into vacation homes, providing a distinctive and genuine experience. Farmhouses are perfect for those wanting a quiet and isolated getaway since they are often found in rural locations surrounded by mountains and farmland.

Country Houses: For those looking for a traditional and genuine lodging alternative, country homes, or casas rurales as they are called in Mallorca, are a popular choice. A distinctive and endearing experience is provided by the many renovated rural houses that have been transformed into vacation homes. Country homes are perfect for travelers looking for a quiet and genuine vacation since they are often found in rural locations, surrounded by tranquillity and nature.

Luxurious Rentals: Mallorca is home to some of the world's most opulent holiday properties. There are several alternatives available for people looking for a high-end and private vacation, from vast and spacious villas to ancient and magnificent manor homes. Private swimming pools, gardens, and outdoor eating spaces are common features of luxury rentals, along with a number of other extras including personal chefs, cleaning, and concierge services.

Beachfront Rentals: Mallorca has some of the most beautiful beaches in the world, and there are many beachfront vacation rentals to choose from. For those looking for a coastal vacation, there are several alternatives available, ranging from tiny and intimate apartments to huge and expansive villas. Beautiful sea views, quick access to the beach, and a variety of water sports are often included with beachfront rentals.

City Rentals: The island of Mallorca is home to a number of stunning towns, including the capital Palma, which has a large selection of vacation rentals right in the middle of the city. For those looking for a city stay in Mallorca, there are several alternatives available, from contemporary and chic flats to elegant and lovely townhouses. City apartments often provide quick access to the area's restaurants, activities, and nightlife.

Mallorca offers a wide range of holiday rentals to accommodate all tastes and price ranges. Mallorca offers everything you're looking for, whether you want a roomy villa with a private pool, a charming apartment in the middle of the city, or a traditional farmhouse in the countryside. In order to discover the ideal vacation rental for your trip to Mallorca, it's crucial to plan ahead and do your homework.

II:

FOOD AND DRINK

Traditional Cuisine

Traditional dishes from the Balearic Islands, Catalonia, and Spain are combined in Mallorca. Fish, shellfish, meats, vegetables, fruits, and other fresh and savory ingredients are abundant on the island and are utilized to make a broad variety of cuisines. Following is a list of some of Mallorca's most well-known regional dishes:

Pa amb oli: This recipe, which is simple yet tasty, is a mainstay of Mallorcan cooking. It consists of garlic-and-olive-oil-rubbed bread that is then covered with a variety of foods, including cured meats, cheese, tomatoes, and peppers.

Sobrasada: Made with ground pork, paprika, and other spices, sobrasada is a sort of cured sausage. It is often eaten spread over toast or crackers and has a soft texture and a deep, smokey taste.

Tumbet: Layers of sliced potatoes, aubergines, and peppers are cooked together with tomato sauce and garlic in this classic vegetable meal. It often has a fried egg on top and is offered as a side dish or a main entrée.

Arroz brut: Similar to paella but with a richer, thicker broth, arroz brut is a robust rice dish. A range of meats, including chicken, hog, and rabbit, as well as vegetables and seasonings are used to make it.

Traditional meat and vegetable stew known as "frita mallorqun" is cooked with pig, liver, potatoes, onions, and red peppers. It is often served as a main meal and seasoned with garlic, paprika, and other spices.

Ensaimada: The sweet pastry known as ensaimada is regarded as Mallorca's national cuisine. A sweet yeast dough is used to make it, which is rolled out into thin strips, formed into a spiral, and baked till golden. It may be filled with a number of ingredients, including cream or chocolate, and is often sprinkled with powdered sugar.

Coca de patata: A sweet potato cake like a muffin, coca de patata. It is often eaten with a cup of hot chocolate or coffee and is prepared using sweet potatoes, flour, sugar, eggs, and aniseed.

A substantial soup called sopa mallorquina is prepared with chicken, veggies, and fideuà (short, thin noodles). It is commonly served with a dollop of aioli and is seasoned with garlic, paprika, and other spices.

Traditional lobster stew known as "caldereta de langosta" is often served on special occasions. It contains lobster, tomatoes, onions, and red peppers, and is sometimes spiced with saffron.

Spanish, Catalan, and Balearic Island cuisines are all present in Mallorca's traditional food. Traditional foods in

Mallorca range from the simple but tasty pa amb oli to robust meat stews and sweet desserts, so there is something for everyone to enjoy. To fully appreciate the variety of tastes and ingredients that make Mallorcan food so distinctive, it is worthwhile to explore the island's local markets and eateries.

Native Specialities

It is worthwhile to sample some of Mallorca's many regional delicacies while you are there since they are all distinctive to the island. Following are a some of Mallorca's most well-known regional specialties:

Ensamada: Known as the most well-known dish in Mallorca, ensamada is a pastry that is exclusive to the island. The ingredients for this coiled pastry include flour, water, sugar, yeast, and pig grease. The dough is formed into a spiral shape, twisted into thin strips, and cooked until golden. Ensamada may be filled with a variety of ingredients, such as cream, chocolate, or pumpkin, and is commonly consumed for breakfast or dessert.

Sobrasada: Made with ground pork, paprika, salt, and other spices, sobrasada is a cured sausage. It is often eaten spread over toast or crackers and has a soft texture and a deep, smokey taste. Sobrasada is a prevalent ingredient in many Mallorcan meals, including the well-known tumbet and frito mallorqun.

Coca de Trampó: Made with a thin crust, tomato sauce, and a variety of vegetables, including tomatoes, onions, and green peppers, Coca de Trampó is a classic Mallorcan meal. It's a well-liked appetizer or snack that often has sobrasada and cheese on top.

Using a variety of meats, including hog, liver, and lamb, as well as potatoes, onions, and red peppers, frit mallorqu is a typical Mallorcan meat and vegetable stew. Garlic, paprika, and other spices are used to season the ingredients while they are cooked in olive oil. It often comes with bread and a glass of red wine as a main meal.

Arrs Brut is a substantial rice dish with a broth that is richer and more delicious than paella. A range of meats, including chicken, rabbit, and pig, as well as vegetables, including tomatoes, onions, and green beans, are used to make it. The rice is given a rich, golden hue by being boiled in a broth comprised of fish stock, saffron, and other spices.

Coca de Patata: A sweet potato cake like a muffin, Coca de Patata. It is often eaten with a cup of hot chocolate or coffee and is prepared from sweet potatoes, flour, sugar, eggs, and aniseed. In Mallorca, people often eat it for breakfast or as a snack.

Tumbet: Layers of sliced potatoes, aubergines, and red peppers are cooked together with tomato sauce and garlic in this classic vegetable meal. It often has a fried egg on top and is offered as a side dish or a main entrée.

Coca de Albaricoque: Coca de Albaricoque is a tart-like sweet apricot cake. It has a buttery crust, apricot jam, almonds, and is often topped with whipped cream.

Cuixot: Made from hog flesh and fat, garlic, and other spices, cuixot is a cured sausage. It is a mainstay of Mallorcan cooking and is often served with bread and cheese as a snack or appetizer.

It is recommended sampling the local delicacies while you are there since they are a delightful and distinctive fusion of tastes and ingredients. from the well-known ensamada pastry to filling stews and desserts.

Prestigious Eateries and Bars

The culinary scene in Mallorca is renowned for its diversity, with several eateries and pubs dishing up delectable fare. The best eateries and nightclubs to visit during your vacation are listed below:

Celler Can Amer is a must-stop for foodies seeking genuine Mallorcan cuisine. It is situated in the village of

Inca. The menu offers meals from the island's farms, including suckling pig, lamb shoulder, and black pork, as well as seafood taken off the coast of Mallorca.

Ca Na Toneta provides a distinctive eating experience that highlights the island's native products. It is located in the charming town of Caimari. Depending on what is in season, the menu varies regularly, but you can expect to find delicacies like roasted aubergines, slow-cooked lamb, and fresh shellfish.

Marc Fosh: In Palma, you may enjoy a modern Mediterranean meal at this Michelin-starred restaurant. The menu offers delicacies like lamb with red pepper and saffron risotto and grilled octopus with black garlic and potato purée.

Sa Foradada: Sa Foradada, a restaurant on a cliff with a view of the sea close to Deià, offers a distinctive eating experience. The restaurant's menu offers grilled fish and beef meals, as well as regional delicacies such tumbet and frito mallorqun, although it is only reachable by foot or boat.

Abaco Cocktail Bar is a must-visit for cocktail aficionados and is situated in the center of Palma's old town. Fresh flowers and fruit are used to adorn the bar, which results in a magnificent aesthetic show. Premium ingredients are used to carefully prepare the drinks.

Sky Bar: The Hotel Hostal Cuba in Palma's rooftop Sky Bar provides breathtaking views of the city and the ocean. Together with a variety of beverages, tapas and small plates are also available at the bar.

La Rose Vermutera & Colmado is a quiet pub in Palma where you can enjoy a range of tapas and small dishes as well as some local vermouth. The tavern offers a nostalgic feel thanks to its antique furnishings and vintage jukebox.

Duke: Both residents and tourists like the stylish pub in Palma. The pub offers a buzzing environment and provides a variety of drinks along with artisan beer and wine.

Cappuccino Grand Café: Visit one of the many Cappuccino Grand Café establishments in Mallorca for a more sophisticated dining experience. The cafés provide a variety of foods, including coffee and beverages, as well as breakfast, brunch, lunch, and supper.

There are several excellent restaurants and pubs there that you may visit while there. There is something to suit everyone's tastes, whether they are craving modern Mediterranean food, traditional Mallorcan dishes, a cool drink, or regional vermouth.

III:

ATTRACTIONS AND ACTIVITIES

Beaches and Water Sports

The idyllic island of Mallorca is home to some of the best beaches and watersports in all of Europe. The best beaches and aquatic activities to try out while you're here are listed below:

Beach de Muro: In the north of the island, this broad, sandy beach is a favorite destination for families. The shallow, quiet water is perfect for swimming and other water activities like paddleboarding and kayaking.

Cala Millor is a well-liked beach on the island's east coast that is renowned for its clean waters and fine white sand. It's a fantastic location for swimming, snorkeling, and sunbathing.

Es Trenc is one of the most well-liked beaches in Mallorca and is a magnificent beach on the island's south coast. It is renowned for its clear waters, beautiful sand, and breathtaking scenery. Paddleboarding, windsurfing, and kitesurfing are examples of watersports.

Cala Mondragó is a beautiful cove and a protected natural reserve that is situated in the southeast of the island. You may go diving and snorkeling there, as well as strolling along the rocky shoreline.

Located in the north of the island, Port de Pollença is a quaint village with a long, sandy beach and calm seas that are ideal for swimming and water sports like paddleboarding and kayaking.

Sailing: With its beautiful, blue seas and more than 300 days of sunlight annually, Mallorca is a great place for sailors. On the island, there are several sailing schools and rental businesses that provide anything from dinghies to lavish yachts.

Scuba diving: With its crystal-clear seas, breathtaking underwater scenery, and plenty of marine life, Mallorca boasts some of the greatest diving locations in all of Europe. On the island, there are a lot of diving schools that provide lessons and accompanied dives for divers of various skill levels.

Surfing and windsurfing: The winds and waves on the island make it a perfect place for these sports. On the island, there are several surf schools and rental businesses that provide gear and instruction to both novice and expert surfers.

Jet skiing is an excellent method for thrill-seekers to explore the island's coves and coastline. There are several businesses that provide guided excursions and jet ski rentals.

Visitors to the island must experience Mallorca's beaches and watersports. Whether you're searching for a laid-back day at the beach or an action-packed adventure on the water, Mallorca has plenty to offer everyone with its crystal-clear seas, breathtaking coastline, and variety of activities.

Cultural and Historical Landmarks

There are many historical and cultural attractions to discover in Mallorca, which has a rich history and culture. The following are some of the top websites to visit while you are there:

Palma Cathedral (La Seu): Constructed between the 13th and the 17th centuries, this magnificent Gothic cathedral is situated in the center of Palma, Mallorca's main city. It has a magnificent rose window, beautiful stone sculptures, and stained glass windows.

Bellver Castle: One of the few circular castles in Europe, this spectacular fortress was constructed in the 14th century and is situated on a hill overlooking Palma. It currently has a historical museum dedicated to Palma and has breathtaking views of both the city and the ocean.

Almudaina Palace: Constructed in the 13th century as a royal home for the kings of Mallorca, this palace is close to the Palma Cathedral. It is now a museum and has Gothic, Renaissance, and Baroque components.

Serra de Tramuntana: In 2011, the UNESCO recognized this mountain range in the northwest of the island as a World Heritage Site. It has beautiful scenery, conventional towns, old terraces, and irrigation systems.

Valldemossa: This scenic community in the Serra de Tramuntana is well-known for its quaint stone homes, winding alleyways, and classic style. Also, it is well-known for the monastery where, in 1838, writers George Sand and musician Frederic Chopin lodged.

Pollentia: A former Roman settlement established in the island's north in the second century BC. It has a theater, a forum, and residential quarters that are all well-preserved.

Sa Llotja: Constructed in the 15th century as a gathering place for merchants, this remarkable Gothic-style structure is situated in the center of Palma. It presently serves as the Fine Arts School and provides a window into Mallorca's lengthy past.

The Museu Fundación Juan March is a contemporary art gallery with artwork by 20th- and 21st-century Spanish and foreign artists. It is situated in Palma.

The cultural hub CaixaForum Palma, which is situated in the city's center, presents a range of exhibits, performances, and seminars on art, culture, and science.

The historical and cultural landmarks in Mallorca provide a fascinating window into the island's colorful history and present. There is something for everyone to discover and enjoy, from magnificent Gothic cathedrals and ancient Roman ruins to lovely towns and contemporary art museums.

Ecosystems and wildlife

Mallorca is renowned for its various natural landscapes, animals, and stunning beaches in addition to its pure seas. The following are some of the island's top natural and animal attractions:

The S'Albufera Natural Reserve is a sizable wetland region in the north of the island that is home to several bird species, including as herons, egrets, and ospreys. The reserve's various paths and viewing platforms may be explored on foot or by bicycle by visitors.

Cabrera Archipelago National Park is a protected region that provides tourists with the possibility to witness rare and unique species of flora and animals, including lizards, seagulls, and dolphins. It is made up of a collection of tiny islands and islets off the southern coast of Mallorca. From Colonia de Sant Jordi, a boat may be used to access the park.

Serra de Tramuntana: A UNESCO World Heritage Site and a well-liked location for hiking, cycling, and rock climbing, this mountain range stretches along Mallorca's northwest coast. It is a must-see location for nature enthusiasts due to its rough peaks, narrow valleys, and breathtaking vistas.

Cap de Formentor: This picturesque peninsula, which is the island's northernmost point, provides stunning views of the sea and the untamed coastline. Many bird species, including as falcons and kestrels, call it home.

A natural reserve, Dragonera Island is home to a diversity of flora and animals, including lizards, birds, and indigenous plant species. It is a tiny island off the southwest coast of Mallorca. Tourists may take a boat journey to discover the island's natural beauties from the port of Sant Elm.

The well-known limestone caverns known as the Caves of Drach are a famous tourist destination and are situated in the eastern region of the island. The caverns' magnificent stalactites and stalagmites, as well as a gorgeous subterranean lake, may be seen on a guided tour.

Mondragó Natural Park: Located in the southeast of the island, this coastal nature reserve provides tourists with the opportunity to see a variety of bird species as well as breathtaking beaches and landscapes. The park has a number of hiking routes and picnic spaces.

Visitors may have a distinctive and intriguing experience thanks to Mallorca's natural scenery and animals. There is something for everyone to explore and enjoy, from marshes and mountains to islands and caverns. Mallorca's natural splendor is certain to create a lasting impact, whether you're a nature enthusiast or simply want to get away from the throng and unwind in a quiet setting.

Entertainment and Nightlife

Particularly in the summer, Mallorca is renowned for its thriving nightlife and entertainment scene. The following are some of the best choices for people seeking a great night out:

There are many pubs, clubs, and restaurants along Palma de Mallorca's Paseo Martimo, a lengthy promenade that runs along the city's waterfront. Both residents and visitors use the location, especially on weekends.

Magaluf: This vibrant resort community on the island's southwest coast is well-known for its nightlife, beach parties, and bars. It is especially well-liked by young travelers seeking a party scene.

El Arenal: El Arenal, a resort community on the island's southeast coast, is home to several pubs, clubs, and music venues. Particularly among German visitors, it is well-liked.

The Jazz Voyeur Club is a stylish venue with live jazz music in the center of Palma de Mallorca. Music aficionados and those seeking a more sophisticated night out frequent this location.

Slot machines, poker, and blackjack are just a few of the activities and entertainment choices available at the Casino de Mallorca in the town of Magaluf. It's a well-liked destination for those seeking a more opulent night out.

Son Amar: This Palmanyola supper and entertainment venue has a range of acts, including as acrobatics, music, and dance. Families and couples seeking a more distinctive and memorable evening out often visit this location.

There are several eateries and pubs at Port Adriano, a marina in the southwest of the island, and there are sometimes festivals and live music performances there as well. For those seeking a laid-back and fashionable evening out, it's a more affluent and refined alternative.

For those seeking nightlife and entertainment, Mallorca has a variety of possibilities, from vibrant beach towns to chic clubs and venues. Anyone can find something to enjoy in Mallorca's nightlife scene, whether they want to party all night long or have a more sedate and classy evening.

Shopping

With a broad range of shopping opportunities, Mallorca is a well-liked shopping destination. The following are some of the best places to shop on the island:

The island's capital, Palma de Mallorca, is the greatest location for shopping. There are several boutiques, department stores, and neighborhood businesses that sell anything from high-end labels to unique handcrafted goods.

Markets: There are several indoor and outdoor markets in Mallorca that offer anything from fresh food to trinkets. The Mercat de l'Olivar in Palma de Mallorca, the Santa Maria del Cami Market, and the Sineu Market are a few of the busiest marketplaces.

Mallorca Fashion Outlet: This outlet retail complex, which is situated in the municipality of Marratxi, has a large selection of national and international brands at reduced costs.

In addition to a variety of high-end stores and luxury boutiques, Portals Nous is also home to a number of premium restaurants and pubs.

Inca: This city is well-known for its leather products, especially its bags and shoes. Visitors may even see the artisans at work in the many stores that sell handcrafted leather goods.

Products made locally: Mallorca is renowned for its ceramics, wine, and olive oil. These goods are available at regional stores and marketplaces, or customers may go directly to the manufacturers for a special shopping experience.

Mallorca has something for everyone, whether you're looking for designer clothing, unusual mementos, or locally made goods.

local shops

Numerous regional markets can be found in Mallorca, where guests can enjoy a distinctive shopping and cultural experience. The following are some of the best markets on the island to visit:

Mercat de l'Olivar: This indoor market, which is situated in the center of Palma de Mallorca, provides a broad selection of fresh fruits, vegetables, meats, and seafood in addition to flowers, spices, and regional goods like olive oil and wine.

The Sineu Market is one of the biggest and oldest markets on the island. It takes place every Wednesday in the town of Sineu. Everything from fresh fruit to handmade goods, apparel, and souvenirs are available to visitors.

Santa Maria del Cami Market: This market, which is held every Sunday in the town of Santa Maria del Cami, is well-liked by both residents and visitors. Many goods, such as fresh food, apparel, and handicrafts, are available for purchase by visitors.

The Inca Market, which takes place every Thursday in the town of Inca, is well-known for its selection of leather shoes, purses, and jackets. Fresh food, apparel, and souvenirs are among the numerous goods that tourists may purchase.

Pollenca Market: This market, which is held every Sunday in the town of Pollenca, sells a range of regional goods, including fresh vegetables, handcrafted goods, and souvenirs. Live music and other entertainment are also available to visitors.

Every Tuesday, the town of Artà hosts the Artà Market, which sells a range of goods including fresh fruit, regional goods, and handicrafts. The town's castle and historic district are also open to visitors.

A terrific approach to learn about Mallorcan culture and customs and to support regional farmers and craftspeople is to go to a local market. The markets in Mallorca provide something for everyone, whether you're seeking for local specialties, one-of-a-kind gifts, or handcrafted goods.

Designer Boutiques

Many designer shops can be found in Mallorca, giving guests the option to splurge on designer clothing and other opulent goods. The following are a few of the island's best designer stores:

Louis Vuitton: The Louis Vuitton shop is situated in the center of Palma de Mallorca and sells a variety of high-end goods, such as handbags, shoes, and accessories.

Hermès: This high-end clothing and accessory retailer has a location in Palma de Mallorca and carries items including jewelry, purses, and scarves.

Gucci: This high-end Italian fashion label has a store in Palma de Mallorca's upscale shopping area that sells a variety of apparel, accessories, and perfumes.

Located in the heart of Palma de Mallorca, Loewe is a high-end Spanish fashion label that sells a variety of upscale apparel, handbags, and accessories.

Escada: This high-end German apparel company has a store in Palma de Mallorca's upscale shopping area where it sells a variety of women's clothes and accessories.

Carolina Herrera: This Venezuelan apparel company has a store in Palma de Mallorca's upscale shopping area where it sells a variety of women's clothes and accessories.

Together with these upscale retail establishments, Palma de Mallorca is also home to El Corte Ingles and Zara, among other high-end department shops. Shoppers seeking designer labels and high-end clothing often go to Palma de Mallorca's upscale shopping area, which is situated around Paseo del Borne and Jaime III.

Mallorca's designer shops provide an opportunity to experience some of the most premium fashion labels in a stunning Mediterranean environment, whether you're wanting to indulge in some luxury shopping or are content to window shop.

T-shirt stores

There are many of gift stores in Mallorca where tourists may buy mementos of the special history and culture of the island. The following are some of the best souvenir stores to visit:

The family-run business Artesania Textil Bujosa, which is based in the municipality of Lloseta, has been making traditional textiles from Mallorca for more than 150 years. Tablecloths, carpets, and other handmade goods are available for purchase by visitors.

Ceramics by Joanna is a store in Alcudia that sells a variety of handmade ceramics created by a nearby artisan named Joanna Santelmo. Plates, bowls, and vases, all with distinctive Mallorcan motifs, are available for purchase by visitors.

In the center of Palma de Mallorca, the lifestyle shop Rialto Living sells a variety of goods, including books, furniture, and clothing accessories. Guests may buy distinctive presents including handcrafted candles, homemade soaps, and decorative items.

El Corte Inglés is a large department store with many sites on the island of Mallorca, including Palma de Mallorca, Playa de Palma, and Puerto Portals. Traditional crafts, apparel, and culinary items may all be purchased as keepsakes by visitors.

Hiper Centro: This sizable shop, which is situated in Palma de Mallorca, sells a range of mementos, including postcards, magnets, keychains, and other items.

Market stalls: The many markets on Mallorca provide a variety of souvenirs, including fresh food, handcrafted goods, and other locally produced goods.

Mallorca's gift stores provide something for every taste and price range, whether you're seeking for a traditional Mallorcan textile, a piece of handmade pottery, or an original piece of home décor.

IV:

PRACTICAL
INFORMATION

Currency and Money Exchange

The Euro is the local currency of Mallorca (EUR). Any of the several banks or currency exchange agencies situated on Mallorca may convert foreign currencies into euros. Here are some pointers about currency exchange in Mallorca:

Banks: In Mallorca, banks normally provide the best exchange rates for changing currencies. Any of the several bank locations on the island will exchange cash for visitors.

Currency exchange offices: Tourist locations are home to a large number of currency exchange offices where visitors may exchange their money. These offices often provide reasonable exchange rates, but to be sure you are receiving the best price, compare rates across offices.

ATMs: Located all around Mallorca, ATMs provide a practical means to withdraw cash in euros. It's a good idea to verify with your bank before going since your bank can impose costs for using international ATMs, so visitors should be aware of this.

Major credit cards like Visa and Mastercard are accepted by the majority of establishments in Mallorca. Before departing, travelers should confirm with their credit card provider that their card will be accepted and that they are aware of any potential penalties or charges.

Traveler's checks: While they're less frequent now, you may still exchange them in banks and exchange bureaus in Mallorca. Traveler's checks may not be accepted by all establishments, so it's a good idea to have cash or a credit card on hand as well.

The procedure of exchanging money in Mallorca is simple, and travelers may choose from a range of choices based on their tastes and requirements. To guarantee you receive the best bargain, check rates and fees for several exchange alternatives.

Language

Spanish is the island of Mallorca's official language, and the majority of the population speaks it. Yet, owing to the island's reputation as a vacation spot, English and German are also commonly spoken, particularly in tourist-oriented regions.

The following advice can help you communicate in Mallorca:

Although if many people in the area speak English, knowing a few fundamental Spanish words can help you interact with people there and better understand their culture. "Hola" (hello), "por favor" (please), "gracias" (thank you), and "bye-bye" are a few helpful expressions (goodbye).

Talk slowly and clearly: To be understood while speaking to natives, speak slowly and clearly. Don't use local terms or slang that others may not understand.

Consider utilizing a translation program, such as Google Translate, if you are having trouble communicating in Spanish. When traveling to more rural locations where English may not be as frequently spoken, these applications can help you translate words and phrases in real-time.

Be respectful: Show consideration and courtesy while speaking with natives.

If someone is having trouble understanding you, try to be patient and refrain from speaking too loudly or in an inappropriate way.

English-speaking tourists find it typically simple to communicate in Mallorca, and many locals are glad to assist tourists who are having trouble doing so. Making your vacation more pleasurable and immersive may be accomplished by learning some fundamental Spanish words and utilizing a translation software.

Safety Advice

With a low crime rate and a good level of life, Mallorca is often a safe place for tourists. Nonetheless, there are a few steps you should take to protect your safety, just as you would in any other vacation location. For tourists to Mallorca's safety, consider the following:

While traveling in Mallorca, be mindful of your surroundings and on the lookout for any possible hazards. Stay in well-lit locations where there are other people present and steer clear of solitary or dark regions, particularly at night.

Secure your valuables: Small-time crimes like theft and pickpocketing may happen in tourist locations. Your cash, passport, and other valuables should be kept in a safe place, such a hotel safe or money belt.

Employ trustworthy transportation: While traveling in Mallorca, use authorized taxis or reputed ride-sharing services. Avoid utilizing unauthorized or unregistered taxis since they could be dangerous and overcharge you.

Beach safety regulations should be followed while enjoying Mallorca's stunning beaches, such as swimming only in specified areas and paying attention to lifeguard advice.

There are numerous stunning hiking and bike paths in Mallorca, but it's crucial to exercise caution and come prepared while exploring these places. Be sure to dress appropriately, have enough of water and food, and be careful of the terrain and weather.

While visiting Mallorca, be respectful to the regional laws and traditions. Refrain from acting in a way that can be considered disrespectful or objectionable by locals, and get aware with their laws and traditions.

local traditions and manners

Visitors to Mallorca who are aware of and respectful of local traditions and etiquette will have a memorable experience. While traveling to Mallorca, take in mind the following manners and customs:

Depending on the degree of acquaintance, it is customary to greet someone with a handshake or a kiss on each cheek. It's courteous to address someone with their official title when you first meet them, such as "Seor" or "Seora."

Lunch, which is normally had between 1 and 3 PM in Mallorca, is the major meal of the day. Usually, dinner is had between 8:00 and 10:00 pm. It is traditional to wait to begin eating until everyone is seated and the host has done so.

While Mallorca is a location with a relaxed dress code, it's still vital to dress correctly when visiting sacred places or going to formal occasions. Most restaurants do not allow beachwear, and it is necessary to cover oneself while visiting places of worship.

Tipping: Although a service fee is often already included in the bill, tipping is not customary in Mallorca. Little change is often left as a thank you for the wonderful service, however.

Language: While English is frequently spoken in tourist areas, Mallorca's official language is Spanish. Learning some fundamental Spanish phrases can help you interact with the people and appreciate their culture.

It's crucial to respect local customs and traditions since Mallorca has a rich cultural past. This entails observing religious customs with respect, such as refraining from taking pictures inside of churches without permission, as well as abstaining from actions that can be seen as insulting or hurtful.

CONCLUSION

Final Thoughts

Mallorca is a wonderfully unique place with the ideal fusion of culture, history, and natural beauty. Mallorca has something for everyone, whether you like the outdoors, are interested in history, or just want to unwind by the beach.

The breathtaking natural beauty of Mallorca is one of its most outstanding features. The island is a haven for outdoor lovers, from the Mediterranean Sea's pristine seas to the rocky peaks of the Tramuntana

Mountains. In addition to sailing, kayaking, and snorkeling on the ocean, tourists may enjoy hiking, bicycling, and horseback riding through picturesque surroundings.

Mallorca's rich history and culture are yet another appealing feature. With signs of human settlement extending back to ancient times, the island has a rich and intriguing history. Ancient ruins, medieval fortresses, Gothic cathedrals, as well as traditional villages and regional markets, may all be explored by tourists to get a taste of Mallorca's distinctive way of life.

Another main attraction for tourists is Mallorca's gastronomy, which offers a wide variety of traditional meals and regional delicacies to try. There is no lack of mouthwatering cuisine to explore, from ensaimadas and sobrasada to fresh fish and paella. Also, a broad selection of wines and liqueurs are available, including the regional Malvasia and Palo.

In terms of lodging, Mallorca has options to suit every need and taste. Choose from opulent resorts and villas, beautiful boutique hotels, or affordable hostels and flats, depending on your budget. Also, there are many of options for holiday rentals, which might be a fantastic choice for families or groups.

Using the public transit system is among the greatest methods to see all of Mallorca. The island is connected to all major towns and tourist areas by a vast network of buses and railways. Visitors may explore the island at their own leisure thanks to the abundance of walking and biking pathways.

Mallorca is renowned for having a thriving entertainment and nightlife scene. There's always something going on on the island, from nightclubs and live music venues to beach clubs and pubs. Yet, when it comes to clothing regulations and conduct in public areas, tourists should also be mindful of regional traditions and etiquette.

The island is certain to make an impact on every tourist with its stunning natural surroundings, voluminous culture, and kind welcome. Mallorca is the ideal location for your next holiday, whether you're seeking for excitement, leisure, or a combination of both.

Tips for a fantastic trip to Mallorca.

Here are some suggestions to make your trip to Mallorca special if you're planning one:

Discover the outdoors: Mallorca is recognized for its breathtaking natural beauty, so make the most of it! Explore the various beaches on the island, the Tramuntana Mountains by foot or bicycle, or go on a boat tour to see undiscovered coves and sea caves.

Take time to visit Mallorca's picturesque towns, historic sites, and traditional markets to fully immerse yourself in the island's culture. Visit Palma's Gothic Cathedral, meander through Pollença's cobblestone streets, or browse the weekly markets for handcrafted goods and souvenirs.

Indulge in some local favorites like ensaimadas (sweet pastries), sobrasada (spicy sausage), and tumbet as Mallorca is known for its delectable cuisine (a vegetable dish). Have a refreshing hierbas or a glass of the local wine to wash it all down (herbal liqueur).

Stay in a distinctive lodging: Mallorca offers a vast selection of lodging options to suit every taste and budget, whether you decide for an opulent resort, a lovely boutique hotel, or a rustic farmstay. For a unique experience, think about staying in a traditional finca (farmhouse) or a former monastery.

Use the buses and trains that Mallorca has to offer; they run efficiently and can take you to all of the main towns and tourist attractions. Hiring a scooter or bike may also be a handy and enjoyable way to get about the island.

Relax and enjoy the nightlife: There are many pubs, clubs, and beach clubs to pick from in Mallorca's vibrant nightlife scene. Have a beverage on a

Palma rooftop bar or party the night away at one of the numerous clubs on the island.

Be cautious to practice responsible tourism since Mallorca's ecology is both lovely and delicate. To guarantee a happy and sustainable travel experience, respect the environment, patronize local companies, and abide by local traditions and etiquette.

You may be sure that your trip to Mallorca will be one to remember by taking these suggestions into consideration.

Printed in Great Britain
by Amazon

25073510R00073